About the author

Bailey Nadeen has written poetry and short stories since she was a child, and has always dreamt of being an author. She was born, raised and still lives in Edmonton, Alberta where she continues to write and perform music and spoken word. She currently attends MacEwan University, majoring in psychology. Bailey uses personal narratives to discuss the ideas of heartache, human nature, and the struggles that come with mental illness. Bailey is a previous winner of the *Words of Hope* University of Alberta Hospital Poetry Contest in 2018. *Growing Pains* is Bailey's first published book.

Crisabel Artacho is an Edmonton based artist who currently attends MacEwan University for Fine Arts. She has always been drawn to the creative world of illustrating. She uses various mediums in her artwork and lives happily with her family and Porky, the cat. *Growing Pains* is the first volume of poetry that she has illustrated.

GROWING PAINS

Bailey Nadeen

GROWING PAINS

Vanguard Press

VANGUARD PAPERBACK

© Copyright 2021
Bailey Nadeen
Illustrated by Crisabel Artacho

The right of **Bailey Nadeen** to be identified as author of this work has been asserted by her in accordance with the Copyright, Designs and Patents Act 1988.

All Rights Reserved

No reproduction, copy or transmission of this publication may be made without written permission.
No paragraph of this publication may be reproduced, copied or transmitted save with the written permission of the publisher, or in accordance with the provisions of the Copyright Act 1956 (as amended).

Any person who commits any unauthorised act in relation to this publication may be liable to criminal prosecution and civil claims for damages.

A CIP catalogue record for this title is available from the British Library.

ISBN 978 1 78465 769 7

Vanguard Press is an imprint of
Pegasus Elliot MacKenzie Publishers Ltd.
www.pegasuspublishers.com

First Published in 2021

Vanguard Press
Sheraton House Castle Park
Cambridge England

Printed & Bound in Great Britain

Dedication

For Michael, who taught me to believe,
for Collins, who taught me to create.
and for the ones who gave me
their hearts to hold,
these poems are for you.

Acknowledgements

This collection of poetry was initially my high school journal. Releasing it into the world is both the craziest and the best thing I have done thus far. I will do my best to be thorough with these acknowledgements.

The biggest thank you is to Jodi Burak, who was my English teacher. I am forever grateful to her for teaching poetry in a way that made me fall in love with it, from rapping Shakespeare sonnets to standing on tables. I owe her everything.

Thank you to my family; my parents, Cassidy and Haley, my siblings. Thank you to Uncle Shawn, who doesn't understand poetry in the slightest and yet comes to every open mic show.

Thank you to Faith Parker, who had the patience to read all the poems I sent her way.

To Janet and Greg Kawchuk, thank you for your constant support, the many chia lattes, and for always believing this book was a possibility.

The Citadel Theater: Doug Mertz and Linette Smith. You both became my mentors and pushed me to be vulnerable in my art to an extent I didn't think I was capable of. Thank you for being the best role models a girl could ask for.

Thank you to Titilope Sonuga, for all the poolside conversation. Your kindness is one in a million.

To the late Shel Silverstein, whose stories have always inspired me; your books will always have a special place on my shelf.

Thank you to Crisabel Artacho, for bringing my stories to life through your beautiful artwork. I couldn't have done it without you.

Last, but not least, thank you to Pegasus Elliot Mackenzie Publishers for this unbelievable opportunity.

Contents

The things I learnt from heartache 17
To the boy wearing a sweater in June 18
Let's be alone together 20
To be a child's art project.................................... 21
I still find it hard to breathe some days.............. 22
I'm not that person anymore 23
Your first love always stays with you................. 24
She's more fragile than most people................... 25
The lamb who fought the lion 27
It's hard to accept carelessness 28
We're not much different, you and I................... 29
To the lady that lives in the flat above mine 31
The boy with the origami heart 33
The first session 34
It became my favorite colour 35
Perhaps that's why she writes poetry 36
The hardest thing I've yet had to do is find a way to get over you... 37
No wonder they all fell for her............................ 39
The man who sold stardust................................... 41
You gave me reasons to shut you out 43
Just because you prepare for goodbye, doesn't mean you're ready for it...................................... 44
It's unpredictable... 45
Shallow people, shallow waters 46

Does love mean all or nothing?........................... 47
Friendships can break your heart too 48
They speak the words that you are too afraid to admit to yourself 50
The lonely St. Valentine...................................... 51
The truth behind indifference............................. 52
Apologies I never said... 53
The artist of his heart... 54
There's love in a look... 55
I had built a library out of people and now I have nothing left to read 56
The man in the moon... 57
It's okay to be a walking corpse some days....... 58
Love is found in all things.................................. 59
Birthday blues 60
Hurtful memories 62
After senior year.. 63
She says he's her anchor, but it's an anchor's job to sink 64
Motherly advice 66
The second session.. 67
Nobody compares.. 69
Why'd you have to go so soon? 70
Life is constantly under construction 71
I'm still learning to be comfortable with you 73
When Sadness visits.. 74
I swallow my feelings like medicine.................. 75

What it's like to love Poseidon 76
Take a risk now and then 77
Stitching myself back together........................... 78
Abracadabra 80
The longer depression stays 81
Love should come with insurance too................ 82
You just have to keep trying 85
I no longer wish on shooting stars...................... 87
A desire for action without consequence 88
Every love story has its Lancelot 89
A lesson that took a long time to learn.............. 90
A boy of many colours.. 91
You were once my everything 92
Every day battles... 93
I hope you find happiness 95
Like father, like son.. 96
Bull in a china shop... 98
You were my constant reminder of good in this world 100
The boy with the empty net............................... 101
November 11th.. 102
So far without you... 104
I'm still not over losing you 106
The light bulb girl 107
Act I... 108
The heart is such a funny thing 109
When the party's over 111

Thank you, Michael 113
You were my lifeline.. 114
The girl who plays with fire 115
God and the Devil 116
The mountains and the wind 119
I hope you read this and know, I no longer care at all.. 120
The drama teacher... 121
Living and surviving are two different things.. 125
One day we were, the next we weren't 126
Life so far 128
If you wonder how I'm doing 130
Your worth is not made by others' opinions.... 133

I used to spend too much time hiding in my head.
Planting dreams and growing seeds in my flower bed.

Too scared to love, too scared to break; afraid to take my shot.
Trying to grow red roses and raise forget me nots.

In order to make flowers grow, you need a little rain.
And pressed between these pages is the truth of growing pains.

The things I learnt from heartache

I don't know the place that you call home or even your first name, but I've memorized your face. You seem to have a type of kindness that is so uncommon, I consider myself lucky to have stumbled upon it.

We exchanged four words when we first met. I had raced up the stairs, in a desperate attempt to beat the oncoming traffic of high school students that would soon fill these empty hallways.

You held open the door.

I smiled. "Thank you."
"No problem," you replied.

As I walked by I noticed your arm. Hand still holding the green door ajar, you were waiting for me to pass through. From the opening of your sleeve I could see that your wrist had horizontal marks on them, like tiny red soldiers all lined up perfectly in a row. I wondered if you were the type of person to spend all night driving on the freeway, wishing your life was as busy as the lanes of traffic passing by. I wanted to ask if you too had nightmares that kept you from sleeping or if you also lost too much too young, but I couldn't find the words. Instead, I walked in the other direction and when I finally realized that perhaps you were in need of someone too, you had disappeared within the crowd of students.

Every day after class, I make sure I'm the first one out. I have this small hope that I'll run into you again, I don't know what I'll say, but it'll be more than a simple thank you.

To the boy wearing a sweater in June

You say you like to be by yourself,
I am like that too.
Although I don't think company would be so bad,
If time were shared with you.

                        Let's be alone together

I often feel like a page ripped from a colouring book, a page that a child had started filling in, but got bored and never finished. Some parts of me are filled with bright blues and greens, scattered across the page in beautiful, random, and majestic patterns. My corners are covered in thick layers of deep purple and sunset orange, perfectly highlighting the smudges of yellow here and there.

Then there are some parts of me that are blank, parts that were left empty, and I do not have the crayons to fill them in. I have always felt unfinished, as though I am never able to see the complete picture. It's like a part of me isn't there, and no matter how hard I try, I cannot fill it in. I desperately need that child to come back and finish what they started.

                                          To be a child's art project

I knew I was in trouble when at first I felt that flame,
When bats flew round inside my stomach each time I heard your name.

Late at night I'd listen to the sound of your heartbeat,
I liked it more than my favorite artist's music on repeat.

I knew I loved you with all I could; you caught me when I fell.
I screamed at you to go away, you walked with me through hell.

After many months of testing trust, your arms became my home.
I'd rather live inside your ribcage than to live my life alone.

I knew I was in trouble when I gave you all my air,
When you took a breath, got up, and left me, suffocating there.

        I still find it hard to breathe some days

I am constantly reminding myself that it's not my job to fix other people. It's not my responsibility to take what is broken and make it whole again.

You do not get to use me to stitch yourself back together then be on your way.

I will not be your personal infirmary.

Do not look to me to fix what you broke.

> I'm not that person anymore

As cliché as it sounds, a part of you still lives in me. It kills me that no matter how many times I try to convince myself that I'm over you, I'm not. The sound of your name still makes my heart race, I still have your laughter saved on the loop track of my memory, and your navy sweater is still hidden in my drawer. I poured everything into you, every crack and flaw, every mistake, every truth. I poured and I poured until I was left empty, but it was okay because you poured every bit of yourself into me. How funny that is to think of now because we're both living with a part of the other that won't go away. Like a roommate ignoring the eviction notice or a guest who overstays their welcome.

                    Your first love always stays with you

In truth, there is no way to break someone gently. Whether you were to toss a vase off of a table or push it off slowly, it breaks all the same. Remember that next time you decide to love her.

    She's more fragile than most people

We each took caution, like we should,
Both our faces straight and sober.
But we were foolish not to see,
That caution would screw us over.

I lost the fight, down and defeated,
The odds never in my favor.
For I had tried my best to fight,
And had challenged the hardest player.

                              The lamb who fought the lion

In hindsight, he never really cared at all.
I'm still trying to get over that.

                        It's hard to accept carelessness

My mind is like a matchstick. Light and warm one moment, burnt out and useless the next. One day it can be filled with bright ideas, such fantastic desires and blinding sensations of passion. The next day it's nothing more than ash, crumbling and used up. I'm a single matchstick in this matchbox world. Our entire lifespan is nothing more than mere seconds of energy to this universe. We're a single stick in a box of millions, waiting for our turn to shed a little light or snap while trying to do so.

    We're not much different, you and I

Lady of the night dressed in black tights,
Runs her face under water, turns off the lights.
The silence grows louder as she lies next to him,
Does she feel herself drowning? Does she know how to swim?

Can her money buy liquor off the top-seller shelf?
Does she drink it alone and talk to herself?
Do you think she regrets it and likes who she is?
Does she ever get lonely in that bed that is his?

She was once very pretty. Her voice now falls out.
Does she look back on life? Does she have any doubt?
I wonder these things as I think late at night.
At least she's surviving, I hope she's all right.

    To the lady that lives in the flat above mine

I fell in love with a paper boy who brought life to my empty pages. He used his fingertips to create poetry across my skin, folding my body like a piece of origami. He treated metaphors like medicine and kept me grounded like a paper weight, he was delicate and cautious; I often found myself getting lost in his words. I fell in love with a paper boy who believed that life got better with time. He took the broken pieces of my heart and glued them back together like papier maché. I consider him to be my first draft, something to be proud of and not forgotten. He is my reminder that not all break up poems need to be sad, not all boys go out of their way to break your heart. Sometimes things just don't work out and that's okay. He made stars out of post it notes and cranes out of old newspapers, I'm thankful for the stories he gave me.

                              The boy with the origami heart

"Not everyone you meet will like you," my therapist reminds me.

I struggle to understand why. "I'm not a cruel person."

"Doesn't matter if you're cruel or not," she explains. "Getting along with people is like finding the right pair of shoes. If they don't fit quite right, you take them off and place them back on the shelf. You mean no offense by not buying them; they just weren't right for you."

The first session

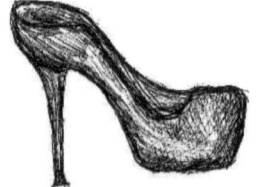 

I've always hated the colour yellow, but when you showed me the house your father left you and explained with such excitement that you were going to paint the dining room yellow because it reminded you of your mother, suddenly, yellow didn't seem so bad.

                                  It became my favorite colour

Her hands shake because her body's filled with so much love and no one to give it to.

        Perhaps that's why she writes poetry

If you're still in love with me, please never let me know because getting over you nearly killed me, and I don't know if I have the strength to do it again. To fall into your arms and have your lips pressed against mine, to memorize the way you say my name, and how you quietly put your hands in your pockets when you're nervous.

It all felt so incredible. It felt so alive.

If I had to endure that heartache again, knowing I'll never be able to kiss your lips or watch your little sister grow up. I don't think I could ever go through that twice. I barely survived the last time, so if you're still in love with me, don't ever tell me so.

The hardest thing I've yet had to do is find a way to get over you

She's the type of girl Billy Joel would write songs about.

                No wonder they all fell for her

Do you remember the man who sailed upon stars?
Who spoke to the moon and travelled to Mars?
The stars they all giggled when he tickled their crown,
And caught all the stardust as it slowly fell down.

He sold it in jars, that stardust he caught.
It was a popular business so he sold quite a lot.
For stardust was rare, it helped people fly.
Without airplanes or wings, they could soar through the sky.

People they fell; they just couldn't perceive,
That in order to fly, you have to believe.
For stardust can get you only half of the way,
Without faith in flight, on the ground you will stay.

So people grew angry and yelled at the man,
And he felt very sad so he made up a plan.
He took all of the stardust and hid it from sight,
The last of it ever on that cold starless night.

                              The man who sold stardust

People get angry when you build walls to keep them out and the irony of that is, in most cases, they were the ones who handed you the bricks.

        You gave me reasons to shut you out

"I mean, I saw it coming," I cry. "A part of me always knew that we'd never end up getting married."

"Then isn't it better that this happened sooner than later?" he asks.

"I suppose," I sniff. "I guess it was just one of those things I knew was going to end, but I needed to hold onto it for just a little bit longer."

>Just because you prepare for goodbye,
>doesn't mean you're ready for it

My darling, you've been warned,
My love is like the calm before the storm.

                                      It's unpredictable

Falling in love with you was like accidentally diving into the shallow end of a swimming pool. I ran off the edge, dove in head first and full of excitement, I couldn't wait to see what lay below.

You let me down. I had always thought there was more to you, that perhaps you were a lost soul searching the waters just as I was. However, you were exactly what everyone said you would be.

I only dip my toes into love now. I'm scared of what will happen if I allow myself to jump in again.

          Shallow people,
            shallow waters

I want to count your freckles, I want to watch you burn.

I miss your steady hand; I pray you'll get your turn.

I'm tired of this tennis game, my heart not knowing how to feel.

Whether today I love or hate you, at least I know my feeling's real.

                    Does love mean all or nothing?

When I was eight years old, I thought that if I rode my bike fast enough down the neighbourhood street that it would lift into the air and I could fly to the moon. Obviously, it didn't work. I tried pedaling as fast as I could, wind in my hair, legs growing numb as I reached the end of the street. One time, my front tire hit a pothole in the road and I flew over the handlebars and crashed into the pavement.

When I told her this story, she laughed and said that it was for reasons like this that I was her best friend. We'd spend hours sitting in coffee shops, telling childhood stories and laughing so much that our stomachs began to hurt. We made jokes that this is how it would always be, us sitting together, drinking coffee, sharing memory after memory. When I got my first car, I drove straight to her house and we spent the night driving around the city, singing at the top of our lungs.

I wasn't prepared for our ending because I never thought there would be an end, but when she chose the admiration of a boy over our friendship I didn't know what to say.

"I've changed," she said, but I hadn't.
I was still the kid who thought I could fly to the moon.

        Friendships can break your heart too

Cherish the ones who speak to you with honesty. If they are brave enough to give you their opinion, be wise enough to listen to it. It takes courage to speak the truth, especially when it does not roll off the tongue so easily. Do not scream at them because their words sting you; you asked for honesty and you got it. Be proud you have a friend who lets you know when you messed up rather than one who shamelessly agrees with you on everything. Be thankful for their caring thoughts and good intentions, do not guilt them for it. You need people like them. Do not forget that.

They speak the words that you are too afraid to admit to yourself

I often think of St. Valentine,
Who speaks in sonnet, poem, and rhyme.
Whose mind is sharp and smile warm,
He promises love will do no harm.

I often think of St. Valentine,
He drinks aged brandy, scotch, and wine.
He lives alone and cries at night,
Underneath the pale moonlight.

I often think of St. Valentine,
Who always watches from the sideline.
His loveliness has lost its hymn,
For we love each other, but who loves him?

                                      The lonely St. Valentine

I often find myself questioning people who say they don't care. I think they're lying. I think they care an awful lot or at least they did at some point. I like to think they're the ones who care the most because if they really didn't care, they wouldn't bother mentioning it. I don't think they're trying to convince you of their carelessness, but rather themselves.

                        The truth behind indifference

Have you forgotten the way we used to be? Dancing across hardwood floors at two in the morning and pretending we had everything figured out. I laugh at how easy we thought love was because now we know much better. Broken hearts are not so easily replaced. I can write you a thousand apology letters, but I know you'll never read them. I can carve our names into trees, hoping it'll remind you of how deeply I cared for you, but it won't undo the hurt I caused.

Everyone talks about how great it is to fall in love, but no one tells you about the clean up and how quick it can get messy. No matter how much you care for someone, it won't fix the things you did wrong.

I'm sorry that I held your hand a little too tightly.

I'm sorry for letting you go a little too quickly.

Apologies I never said

She spoke to him with words of hope, in bright warm colours he thought he would never see.
She had taken his crippling sadness and turned him into beauty; turned him into art.

> The artist of his heart

My heart skips a beat the moment we meet and I know from the way you smile, you're going to cause me a lot of heartache.

>There's love in a look

It was a hard lesson to learn that people don't like being left behind. I always intended to come back, but I see now I had failed to tell them that. I guess that's why you can't treat people like books; put a bookmark in them when you have other things to do and then come back when there's more free time. People don't like that. I never understood why because I never truly meant to go away. I just needed time alone for a while, time to myself and to my thoughts, time to figure things out.

I always expected to return and continue from where we had left off, that there would just be a bit more to catch up on. Read a few new chapters and be on the same page again, and that everything would be okay. I had no idea that once you put the book down, you cannot continue to read the story. People aren't like books. You can't set them on a shelf and expect them to stay there. I know that now.

> I had built a library out of people and
> now I have nothing left to read

I sometimes dream of a midnight man,
Drenched in moonlight, rose in hand.

Soft music plays and we dance all night,
Our movements godlike, our feet take flight.

He whispers words I long to hear,
He speaks so softly, I have no fear.

The song plays on, and the stars shine bright.
They sing and sparkle with all their might.

He takes my waist, a move he makes,
But before a kiss, alone I wake.

                                        The man in the moon

I've always hated the question, are you okay? I never take the time to look at myself and actually wonder whether I am or not. I'm focused on surviving; I go about each day telling myself to do things in a step-by-step manner. I've gotten decent at being productive again and questioning if I'm truly all right gets me thinking. I've been doing so well by not doing that.

It's okay to be a walking corpse some days

You cannot hide yourself when it comes to love.

You are a cave and love is a miner. It will dig and dig until it finds the deepest parts of you.

You cannot hide yourself when it comes to love.

You are a book and love is a scholar. It will stay up all night and study your every paragraph.

Love will take the broken parts of you and turn them whole again.

One day, you will be grateful that you stumbled upon it.

Love is found in all things

I don't know if I'm the only one who feels a sense of dread when it's their birthday or who freaks out when they're asked to make a wish and have no idea what to wish for. I miss my old birthdays like when I was six years old and invited the entire class to the spray park. I wished for a blue bike with purple streamers and a silver bell.

Now whenever someone cries "Happy birthday!" it really sounds like they're saying "Wow, you're already another year older and you haven't accomplished anything! Anyways, here's this gift of bath salts you can have."

My sister calls it the birthday blues. It's when turning another year older feels more like a disappointment than anything else. It's seeing the candles on the cake and knowing that each one represents a year you wasted; time that you can never get back.

"Make a wish," they say, placing the chocolate frosted cake before me.

I close my eyes. I wish to be happy, I think and blow.

As I watch the wax melt down the candles and bits of smoke rise, I can't help but feel disappointed; it's just another case of the birthday blues.

                                      Birthday blues

"I remember her. Of course, I remember her, but it hurts to," I whisper.

"If it hurts then you need to let her go," he replies.

I shake my head. "I can't."

"Why the hell not?" he cries.

"Because as much as it hurts, it's the only thing I have left of her, and I'd rather feel that than nothing at all."

Hurtful memories

You're only friends with some people because you see them five days a week. The only thing holding your friendship together is helping the other with biology homework and figuring out a tough math problem. It's reviewing an English project and having your world flipped upside down when you realize that The Lion King is based off of Hamlet. It's sitting at a cafeteria table in the morning and copying down a last minute assignment you forgot about. It's borrowing five dollars and swearing to pay them back, but never do. It's whispering the answer in class when the teacher calls on them unexpectedly and it's covering for each other when you're late.

At graduation, you'll sit together and clap politely when they walk across the stage with their diploma held tightly in hand. It's hugging them on the last day and promising to keep in touch, but you never do. Maybe you talk for the first few months, but then you both get busy, only ever having time for small talk. Then it's running into them at the grocery store. They're in university right now and you still owe them five dollars.

After senior year

Her smile always shone of passion and his heart deep like the sea.
She was his muse, her voice so soft; her heart was filled with glee.

Two halves of a whole is what people said. They were meant to be together.
Yet it's always tough to see ahead when the sea has such bad weather.

For he often took his anger out on her with no reprieve,
And blinded by the love of him, she couldn't dare to leave.

They asked her of his awful deeds, she shooed them all away.
Swore he atoned for every bruise, he rarely got that way.

So they never bothered to ask again and the cycle kept repeating,
Of a messed up man and his love sick wife who took on a daily beating.

Purple, black, brown, and blue, darling bruises aren't nice art.

Yet it's been so long she cannot tell abuse from love apart.

She clings to him so very tightly and he only drags her down,
I hope she sees the mess she's in or else she'll surely drown.

> She says he's her anchor, but
> it's an anchor's job to sink

After three months of still not being over him, my mother said, "Tie back your hair, drink some vodka, and get the hell over it."

                                              Motherly advice

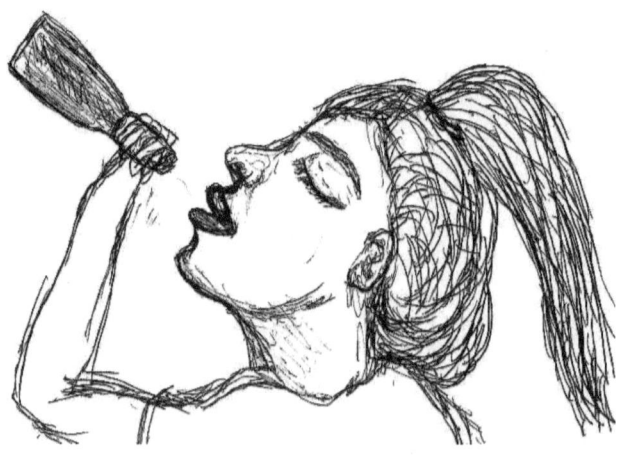

There's this exercise used in therapy where you sit in front of an empty chair and have to imagine a person that caused you pain sitting across from you. I pictured him with his messy hair, wearing that green sweatshirt he always liked. I wanted to reach across the table and rip the smile off of his face. I wanted to scream, cry, kick, and yell, anything to get his attention and make him realize that I'm still hurting after how he left me. I wanted to take his broken promises and shove them down his throat, make him realize how hard it was for me to swallow his lies. How they sometimes still find their way back up to my mouth and that he's the reason why I always pause before I speak.

My therapist asked me what I'd do if I actually were to run into him. I imagine I'll see him across a crowded room and that I'd pass through the people the same way that Moses split the sea and his eyes would meet mine. I'd stare at him the way a wildfire stares at a forest, I haven't planned out what I'd say and maybe I wouldn't speak at all.

I often wonder how many boys hide their abuse with saying their ex girlfriends are crazy. I bet he sits and laughs and jokes about his past relationships, I bet he says that I'm the one who had issues when people ask what happened between us. I'm trying to get better at not caring what people think of me; I'm learning to let go of the pain that I keep holding onto. When I sit in front of that empty chair I tell him that I hope he's not the person that he used to be, I pray he's gotten softer and for now, I think that is enough.

The second session

I do not have the right to compare every new lover to you, but I do anyway. I look into his eyes and I know that they are not as green as yours, as soft as yours, as kind as yours. He may do for me the same things you once did, but it doesn't feel the same. I don't think it ever will.

He has to ask me what I want, whereas you already knew.

He has to ask me if I love him, whereas you never had to.

Nobody compares

I'm sorry, but I had no clue
That sadness had filled up your brain
And made a mess of you.

                       Why'd you have to go so soon?

I'm growing tired of trying. Do you know what that's like? It's being a kid and building a tower with blocks and once you think you're finished, someone comes and knocks it down. You pick up the fallen pieces and build the tower again; it crashes down. You build it just as you did before and it gets knocked down all the same. It becomes a type of routine and without thinking; you just build the tower over and over again. Every time hoping it's going to stand. It doesn't. You keep trying to build it up even though you know it'll come crashing down anyway. It's like being stuck in a type of repetitive hell, a video replaying itself, or skipping to the end of a book before the story even begins.

                Life is constantly under construction

When he first told me about you, my stomach dropped and I knew this would be it. He talked about you like you were his reason to get up each morning, which you were, but it didn't hurt any less. As months rolled by you became his favorite topic of conversation.

To the new girlfriend I've never met, I know red is your favorite colour and that you asked for new skates for Christmas. I know you go to church every Sunday and got into university on the first try. Every detail he told me about you stuck in my head like a song that's always played on the radio, I know every lyric and it's painful to try and forget.

It's hard to hate someone I know so much about.

My heart broke the day he told me he kissed you, I said I was happy for him; it's the worst lie I've ever told.

    I'm still learning to be comfortable with you

If there's one thing I've learned, it is that when Sadness comes knocking, all I can do is say, "I see you." Acknowledge her presence, and spend some time with her. I don't push her away or ask why she came. I'm not afraid of her and because I'm not afraid, I'm able to close the door.

When Sadness visits

I want to tell you that I love you,
But I know you'll run away.
Because every person I've held close,
Decided not to stay.

It's tough to say I care for you,
Those words are hard to find.
So I'll keep an image of your smile,
Tucked away in mind.

It seems to be that you're the one,
But I've said those words before.
Instead I'll keep them to myself,
Because love's a sickness, not a war.

                I swallow my feelings like medicine

You came into my life and nearly knocked me off my feet.

It was almost like I was a kid again.

We were standing in the ocean, holding hands and jumping waves. I couldn't stop laughing. The taste of salt water burned my lips, the sun tickled my back. Every time a wave would come, you'd yell "jump."

I'd obey.

This became repetitive.

You would cry out for me to leap and I'd ask "how high?"

It came to a point where my knees would buckle each time I landed, I was growing tired because being with you became painful for me.

You came into my life and nearly knocked me off my feet. I'm lucky to have good balance.

                        What it's like to love Poseidon

You hold onto fear like a drunk holds onto his bottle and you still have the nerve to wonder why things never go your way.

                        Take a risk now and then

They told me to throw away your sweater, but I couldn't bear to part with it. This was not because I wanted to hold onto what little piece of you I still had left. No, I kept it to prove that I'm over you. I know how backwards that must seem, but every time I take that sweater out and look at it, I feel distant towards it, distant towards you. Each time I take it out, I feel less and less every time. Some days I'll put it on, this helps me realize that it is no longer your sweater, but just a piece of fabric. I think people should know that moving on doesn't always mean letting go.

                               Stitching myself back together

There once was a magic man at the summer town fair,
He would spin in his cloak then, poof, no longer there.

The crowd would all clap as the man took a bow,
And all people, all ages, asked the same thing: how?

He'd do other tricks too with a deck of gold cards,
Charming with people and would send his regards.

Watch him saw ladies in half and sew them together,
Make rabbits appear from his hat of old leather.

I know how he does it. He wears a good mask,
And when people aren't looking, he takes out a flask.

He drinks a bottle of potions after every damn show,
Alone with his magic and nowhere to go.

In an old tattered suit with some tricks up each sleeve,
But you wouldn't have guessed because it's his job to deceive.

                                        Abracadabra

I can't tell if it's getting better or if I'm just getting used to it.

                        The longer depression stays

I'm not quite sure how we got here, tangled in a mess of gentle hands and heavy breathing. Both of us knowing that love had left long ago, yet still holding onto each other as though pressing our bodies closer together would somehow stitch up everything that tore us apart. I wish I could still call you mine, but people aren't property. Even if they were, you were never mine to claim anyway.

                    Love should come with insurance too

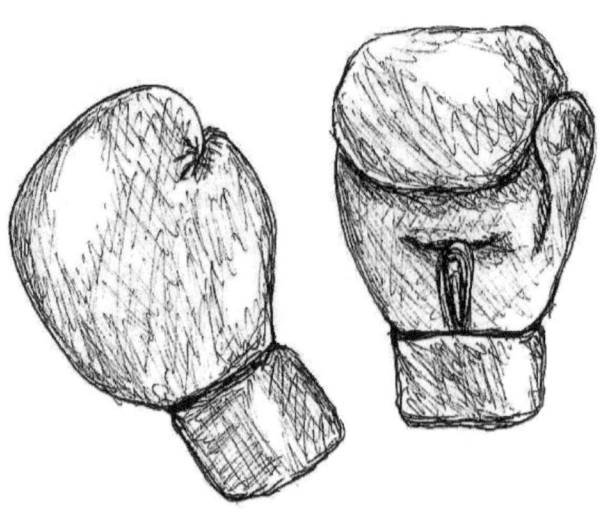

"Can I ask you a question?" I whisper.

He raises his eyebrows.

"If things are so bad, why do you keep trying?" I ask.

"Because," he replies. "I'd rather die fighting in the ring than sitting in the locker room. I'd rather go out punching than to go out without a fight."

                                        You just have to keep trying

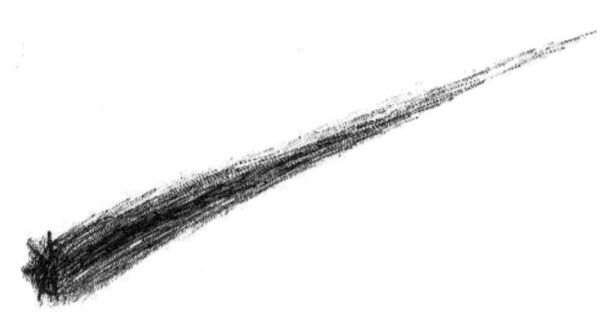

I think I'll blame it on the stars for why things didn't work out between us. Perhaps they were jealous of the way we looked at each other, or maybe it's because we stole the attention away from their shining light with our midnight giggles. It could be that they found out we no longer desired to explore the universe because we already saw galaxies in each other's eyes.

They decided we must be put to an end.

Now, I bet they tell stories of us up in the heavens, of a boy who could never speak his mind and of a girl who often felt too much; for the stars sleep very little and stories are a way to pass the time. So, if you look up in the night sky, I hope you are reminded of me and of what we had because surely the stars haven't forgotten.

                      I no longer wish on shooting stars

I want to be drunk without the hangover and in love without the heartache.

    A desire for action without consequence

He thought of all the things to say,

"Goodbye."

"Goodnight."

"I love you."

Without the courage of a thousand men,
Silence was all he could muster.
So, he watched you leave, you walked away.

You had chosen someone prouder.
And he finally understood why
King Arthur wept for Guinevere.

                    Every love story has its Lancelot

There is a difference between being kind and letting people walk all over you.

A lesson that took a long time to learn

My lover sees in shades of green,
The good, the bad, the in between.
He often speaks with his hands,
Holding mine and making plans.

My lover thinks in shades of blue,
He always knows just what to do.
Holds me close, kisses my head,
Leaves on a light when we're in bed.

My lover lives in shades of white,
He'll never admit he's not all right.
Because if trouble ever does come knocking,
He'll lock the door and keep on walking.

       A boy of many colours

If they ask me if I thought you cared for me, I'll smile and say, "I think so." I'll look back at the time we spent together and go over the type of person I knew you were. How you never bought me flowers, but never forgot to say goodnight. How you were always late coming over, but never felt rushed to leave.

If they ask me if you loved me, I'll have to take a deep breath. They don't understand that people like you wouldn't do the things you did without love. They wouldn't drive over in the middle of the afternoon to help hang up Christmas lights or take pictures of me on long walks. They wouldn't remind me to take my medication or listen to my favorite artist on a constant loop.

If they ask me if I loved you in return, I'll bite my tongue. If they only knew you half as well as I did, they'd be lucky to be half as in love with you as I was.

You were once my everything

My doctor told me to treat a panic attack like a war zone. Think of friends as the medics because we both know they would volunteer to guard the front lines if I asked them to. He explained that fighting mental illness was the same as preparing for war. You never know the enemy's strategy, but you must always be prepared for an attack. I'll put on my uniform, tell myself to be brave, and tie up my boots. I'm ready to fight another day. I treat positivity like ammunition; I constantly try to kill a bad thought with a good one. I'm still trying to be a worthy soldier. I want to make my family proud, but when I hear the gunfire and watch the ground around me shake; everything I once thought I knew about war is lost. I have shaky hands for a soldier. I have a soft stomach. It's hard some days to believe I'll make it to another day, but I remember I have family back home that's counting on me. I have a country that I have to make proud. I don't have time to start giving up.

                                            Every day battles

I miss the friend you used to be; the shy boy who wore grey sweaters and always spoke a little too quietly. I miss those late night drives and how you always had a reason for why life was worth living. I will sometimes bring you up in conversation just to see how you are doing and if things have gotten any better. I hope they have.

I believe cruelty grew on you like a sickness. It took the good parts of you and made them so dizzy that they couldn't tell right from wrong any more.

The last day I saw you were at the grocery store. You were stocking shelves and watched me walk by. I smiled at you, you ignored me, and the rejection felt like a black hole had grown inside of my stomach and was sucking away all the happiness that I had grown there.

I realized that day, you no longer cared about me, and I'm still trying to live with that.

>I hope you find happiness

You gave him a wool blanket and sent him on his way,
Signed legal papers and didn't care that you sold his life away.
He raised you from a baby and you were his shining son,
He taught you how to walk and skate, and how to shoot a gun.

Taught you how to drive a standard up an icy hill,
Gave to you his old piano in his dying will.
But, never do you go to see him because you are all grown,
Work the law firm, get big cheques, have a family of your own.

His birthday passed three days ago, I know he wished for you.
To see the man you have become and your baby dressed in blue.
You never call to talk to him or send a picture now and then,
And he'll still talk about the day when he'll see his son again.

You'll never have to visit him because he died last night,

So here's the blanket that you gave to him when he left without a fight.
Keep it in your dresser drawer until the very day,
When your loving son you trust so much decides to give you away.

        Like father, like son

The Mythbusters once let an actual bull into a china shop. They wanted to see whether or not the statement was true and if the bull would destroy everything in its path.

My mother always told me that I would bring chaos wherever I went. I carried that burden through most of my teenage years. After every argument and failed relationship, I thought back to what she said. I would always be a walking form of destruction.

I'm clumsy when it comes to love; it is a poem my hands are too shaky to write. I find that trust is an Olympic sprinter and I have never been that fast at running. I keep telling myself that not every conversation I have has to end in an argument, I'm still learning that every fight doesn't need to be fought.

When they let the bull into the china shop, at first, it stayed rather still. Then, ever so gently it made its way through the aisles, not breaking a single thing. It gives me hope that perhaps someday, that will be me.

Bull in a china shop

I think that's why so many people fell in love with him; he was the type of happy you always dreamt you could be.

> You were my constant reminder
> of good in this world

He always had to help the ones who could never help themselves. He was a boy trying to save butterflies from a tornado, frantically running around, swinging a net, trying desperately to catch them. I believe he helped them for the sake of having someone to help, as if being there for someone, for anyone, gave him a sense of purpose. He never saw the storm in the distance. He never saw the approaching danger, until the day he was swept away.

The boy with the empty net

Upon a field, beneath the sky,
He ducks below as bullets fly.
As soldiers cry and more men die,
Praying to last just one more day.

He holds his rifle tight in hand,
He fights upon an unknown land.
His country had told him to stand,
And that staying home was cowardly.

He thinks of the girl he left behind,
And hopes to God she'll someday find
The courage to seek some peace of mind,
If he does not return back home.

The sound of fire shortly lightens,
The grip around his trigger tightens.
He sees the other men are frightened,
Someone must lead them on.

He cries to them, "Please, be brave.
Men are to war its hungry slave.
To freedom our lives we gave.
Get up, let's keep on going."

He pulls the trigger, but cannot look
At the bodies of the lives he took.

He tallies the numbers in God's book,
That he keeps inside his pocket.

And today, he watches the parade,
Remembering the price he paid.
The sacrifice his brothers made,
To keep the world from dying.

So if you see him, say thank you,
For doing what he chose to do.
For fighting there to give to you,
The freedom you take for granted.

         November 11th

I want to write the words I am successful on the side of every building I see. I want to watch you walk past it and be reminded that you're the one who gave up on me and that right now, I'm doing better without you. I want to scream from the rooftops, post it on billboards, and tell anyone who will listen that I'm doing fine. I'm doing great. I don't need you anymore.

No one teaches you the difference between being alone and being lonely. There's no *Getting Over Heartache for Dummies*. You will have to force yourself to go to coffee shops and grocery stores, any excuse you can make to be around other people. You will dodge behind your best friend the first time you see him in public and you will cry afterwards because he's looking great and you didn't even bother to shower that day. You will consider adopting a cat, don't do that. Then you'll download Tinder, go on a few first dates and realize that you're better off being by yourself.

Success is champagne that I have to remind myself not to get drunk off of. There's a difference between knowing what you want and parading what you have. I don't need billboards and spray

paint. I want you to know that I'm doing okay without me having to say it.
I know that I'm all right now and that's all that matters.

                        So far without you

When you talk about her, I do my best to smile.

Yet all I can think is,
That should have been me.

That should have been me.

That should have been me.

                                        I'm still not over losing you

I told myself that I had flicked my feelings off. I was convinced that if I refused to acknowledge that love exists, it would get bored and walk away. However, love likes to linger; it does not get bored. I used to believe that heartache was a light bulb powered by longing and I swore that I would never find myself beneath that light again.

Then you came along and taught me that I was never the one in control of the switch.

The light bulb girl

Depression is a theatre that I seldom seem to find my way out of. I'll spend days at a time picking up fallen objects and stuffing dirty costumes into a laundry bin, but they always seem to find their way back to the floor. I often second guess if I have the strength to pull back the curtains and let the spotlight shine through. It hovers on the stage of this one act show that I'm positive no one would waste their time watching. I'm still trying to convince myself that there is an audience behind these curtains; they may just have to wait a little while longer for the show.

Act I

I chose to love him. He chose to love her.

If there is a greater tragedy than loving someone and them not loving you in return, it is one that the world does not yet know.

>The heart is such a funny thing

When the party's over and the music plays no more,
When all the guests have gone away and there are shoeprints on the floor.
After all the champagne's gone and you can't see straight ahead,
Take all your drunken thoughts and tuck them into bed.

When all seems lost or broken and things are not as bright,
When it's quiet and you're all alone in the middle of the night.
Remember every step you took got you where you are,
And if you ever need someone to call, help is never off too far.

I know you're tired of it all, but there's work that still needs done,
Pick up your things and shake the dust, for it has only just begun.
There will be more parties and more dancing where things are not so sad,
You need a balance in your life between the good things and the bad.

When the party's over

It's okay to depend on people, people need depending on anyway.

> Thank you, Michael

My best friend once told me, "Being hopeful for the future is hard, especially when it doesn't look so hopeful. All I ask of you is to be curious enough about the days ahead to want to stick around."

I think about that at least once a day and it reminds me that perhaps curiosity is enough.

You were my lifeline

She often lived in chaos, between the embers and the flame.
Her sparks would burn your fragile tongue,
If you ever spoke her name.

With hair as dark as night and a heart as cold as stone.
You'd be better off to walk away,
Go live happy and alone.

She burns the ones she cares about, no doubt she'd hurt you too.
Leave you choking on the ashes
Of the things you thought you knew.

Her smoke will fill your weary lungs; your heart will fill with doubt.
For the girl who plays with fire,
Has a lot to figure out.

      The girl who plays with fire

Tell me the story of when God and the Devil played chess.

They talk about the good old days when everything wasn't a competition. The Devil cheats and God lets him, he knows that he's going to win anyway. They chat about the troubled souls, God wants to fix them and the Devil wants to sit back and see how it plays out.

"People are not part of a play," God says.

"Then why were we cast as directors?" the Devil asks.

The game continues in silence; God counts his blessings and the Devil twiddles his thumbs.

"Check," the Devil cries, but God avoids the trap because that's just who he is.

They talk about the chaos in the world. God thinks there is too much of it and the Devil believes chaos makes the world go round.

"Chaos builds character," the Devil states.

"Checkmate," God whispers.

The Devil screams.

They reset the board and play again.

God and the Devil

My father always said that some people were built like mountains and others like the wind. It's bad luck to fall in love with a mountain because their minds are rough and rigid; they're grounded and set in their ways. He explained that people like me were like the wind. We are free spirited and destined to reach new heights. Mountains are made to stay in one place whereas the wind must always keep moving.

I fell in love with a mountain once and the way he stood so tall and proud. It's bad luck to fall in love with a mountain because they never change their minds. They weigh down your good ideas and throw hurtful words that make you feel like you're caught under an avalanche.

It took a while for me to learn that you can't move a mountain, there is no middle ground for them. They will never meet you halfway because they believe the best place to be is on the top and they will never step aside, you will have to go around them. I learnt the hard way that you can't force yourself through a mountain. No matter how reasonable you may be, they will never agree with you. Don't waste your time on mountains; they're not worth the climb.

>The mountains and the wind

I knew I was over you when I could look you in the eyes and feel absolutely nothing. I didn't reminisce over the friendship we had or feel angry for what you did to me. I didn't forgive you for the sake of your reputation, but for the sake of mine. I like to believe that is what they call closure.

> I hope you read this and know,
> I no longer care at all

There was this teacher at my school called Mr. Collins. He was about five foot seven, weighed approximately a hundred and thirty pounds, and had a tattoo of a flying narwhale on his right bicep. He wasn't like other drama teachers. He had a mini fridge filled with Coca-Cola in his classroom and despised anything remotely related to Shakespeare. He passed through the hallways the same way Jesus had walked on water and we worshipped the ground he walked on.

First period was always my favorite. We would pour into the drama classroom; not wanting to miss a second of what the lesson had to offer. We'd sit ourselves in one of the many mismatched couches and armchairs below the torn up posters of past productions and wait. Mr. Collins would take attendance and every kid would chime in with pride when he called out their name. He'd then clap his hands together, tell us all to stand up and the class would begin. We'd spend hours diving into scenes of mystery and romance, becoming characters that we never thought we could be. The boy with the stutter became a dashing silver-tongued villain, the girl with a name nobody could pronounce morphed into an exotic goddess.

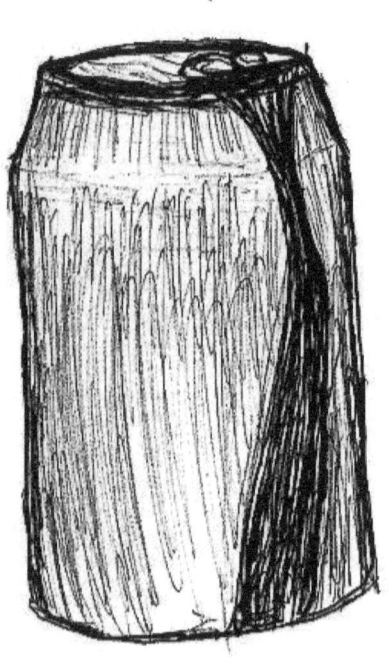

Mr. Collins took our voices and made us believe that we were a song impossible to ignore. The girl who always had a knack for helping people is in school currently to become a doctor, the boy who once made short films in the cafeteria is now a movie director; and I, always scared of public speaking; do spoken poetry.

Mr. Collins took a group of misfits and turned them into scholars, actors, nurses, scientists, and writers. He saw potential in every one of us and took the time, not only to learn our passions, but to help us pursue them. Every time we heard the crack of a can of Coca-Cola being opened, we knew a wave of great advice was coming.

No matter how messy our lives got, there was never a problem that an hour and thirty minutes in the drama room couldn't solve. It was thanks to Mr. Collins that we pushed through three years of heartache, depression, and teenage chaos. I will never forget those stage productions, how everything always came together at the last minute and afterwards, the parents in the audience would clap for us like we were the latest hit on Broadway. Mr. Collins taught us to live our lives with purpose; to find what made us want to get up each morning and never let that passion go. He was my hero and I hope someday, I'll be able to return the favour.

The drama teacher

We're often too focused on trying to survive.

We forget about living.

We forget we're alive.

    Living and surviving are two different things

There's always going to be a part of me that will never fall out of love with you. You can't tell me that a part of you doesn't feel the same because you still hug me the way you used too; a little too tight for a little too long. Your arms wrap around my waist like a child holding tightly onto a daydream, scared to let go for the next second it might disappear.

You were once everything I thought I wanted. I wished for you on every birthday until you were mine.

It's been a year since we broke up and you're with someone else now. It leaves me wondering if there was something different I could have done to make you stay. If there was something I could have said that would have changed your mind.

I guess I'll never know what we could have been. I tell myself that I'm lucky to still be a part of your life, lucky that you still trust me to keep your secrets. I keep them hidden inside my ribcage, it hurts sometimes when they try to claw their way out; it's love that keeps them at bay. They won't be escaping any time soon.

One day we were, the next we weren't

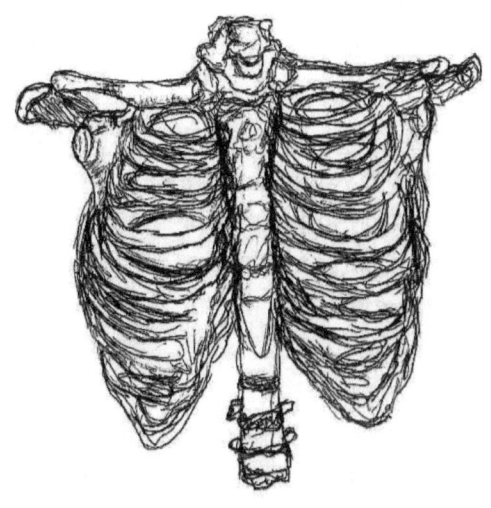

I've spent years trying to drown my demons, but they always find a way to survive. They hide behind every *I'm okay* and sit in shotgun on late night drives. Sometimes I feel like a jack-o-lantern, a smile carved into my face.

The first time he noticed the scars on my wrist, he asked me who put them there and I didn't know what to say. I wanted to tell him that my depression is a home wrecker who refuses to pay his child support; instead he shows up every now and then spewing insecurities like a broken fire hydrant. He gambles with my mind, trading in happy memories for thoughts of childhood trauma. He gets drunk off my bad ideas and thinks it's funny when I can never say what's really wrong.

I've realized recently how addictive depression can be because happiness always feels like a set up for disappointment. When I told my therapist this, she said that even she couldn't drown her demons, but she learned to live one step ahead of them. She explained that it's okay that they sit in the car as long as you're the one who's driving. You just have to turn up the music, nod your head, and remind yourself that everything will be all right.

Life so far

I no longer listen to songs that make me sad. I don't check my phone and hope to see your name appear across the screen. I'm getting better at participating in life again and it's the hardest thing I've ever tried to do. I'm learning that I don't need you to be happy; I don't need anyone's approval except my own. I'm doing what I want to do, dancing in rainstorms and singing along to the radio.

I take myself to movie theaters and coffee shops, I sit and watch the people, I wonder if they're trying like I am and if they're happy with how they're doing so far. I don't think about you anymore and I'm glad that I don't. I read books that I never thought I'd read. I go for walks and no longer care if I step on the cracks between the pavement. I know what I want in life and I don't need your permission to have it.

If you're looking for an explanation on how I'm doing in life, this is it. Things are a lot better now that you're gone. If you feel guilty about what you did and you text me, I promise you I will ignore it. I no longer go back to the people that hurt me; I don't crave your apologies. I don't hold grudges, but I know better than to give people like you second chances. I can live without you and perhaps you think that's unfair, but it's such a nicer way to live.

I just need you to know that life is so much better when you don't set your expectations on others opinions; I think that's something you still need to learn. You shouldn't have to act up in order to get attention, you need to learn that you may not always be the most talented one in the room, and you have to be okay with that. I won't say that I hope you're happy, I just hope you learn and I hope you change, I think that's the best you can think for anybody.

If you wonder how I'm doing

It's hard to find out who you are,
Without knowing who to be.
It's hard to live behind closed doors,
With the longing to be free.

You never know what's in store,
If you stop caring what people think.
For a boat stuck in the ocean,
Has its choice to sail or sink.

      Your worth is not made by others' opinions

www.ingramcontent.com/pod-product-compliance
Lightning Source LLC
LaVergne TN
LVHW091556060526
838200LV00036B/870